PRIME DIRECTIVE

Poems by
Bryan D. Dietrich
2nd Edition 2018
1st Edition Trade Paperback 2011

All Rights Reserved

DARK RECESSES PRESS
657 Craigen Road
Newburgh, Ontario
Canada K0K 2S0

Edited by Rich Ristow
Cover Art & Design by Heather Boyce-Broddle

Library & Archives Canada ISBN
978-1-988837-02-4

ALSO BY BRYAN D. DIETRICH

The Assumption
Love Craft
Universal Monsters
Krypton Nights
The Monstrance

Acknowledgments

Thanks to Rich Ristow and Needfire Press for originally plucking my poem from the ether.

Thanks to Heather Boyce-Broddle for her out-of-this-world cover design, to P. Michael Evans for the author photo, to William Shatner for his kindness and generosity, and to Shooting Stars and the Trek Expo in Tulsa for providing the opportunity.

Thanks to Gene Roddenberry for imagining a modern myth, to the creators of the JVC Videosphere for designing the space helmet TV on which I watched it as a kid, and to Jerry Holt, my Teacher, for offering new and astonishing ways of reading stars.

Thanks to Jimmy Don Burnett for teaching me how to build a tricorder, to Harlan Ellison for providing the requisite stone knives and bear skins, and to Roger Waters and Jean Michel Jarre for supplying the soundtrack.

Thanks to my family for letting me grow up geek—my father for all those other worlds, my mother for this one, and my sisters for encouraging me to go boldly. A special thanks to Beverly who has become my father's Guardian of Forever.

Finally, thanks to Gina and to Nick for initiating me into their alien culture, to E.B. and Doris Greenway for welcoming this particular alien among them, and to Newman University and the IAFA, grand federations that make my mission possible.

Dedication

For My Son, Nick.

TABLE OF CONTENTS

Introduction
Alluding to a Contemporary Myth

If *Prime Directive* were a work of prose, its very *Star Trek* nature would rub up against a strong stigma. To some, it would be easily dismissible as 'fan fiction.' Even as a book-length poem, an intellectually lazy reader might try to dismiss it, passing it off as fan-inspired writing not worthy of 'serious' attention. It has happened before, with Jeff Burk's Eraserhead Press novel, *Shatnerquake.* Nevermind Burk's obvious satire, not to mention the absurdist qualities marking both Burk's writing and the bizarro fiction genre in general. Burk was doing something more than 'playing with the toys' both *Star Trek* and William Shatner's public persona offer. In his own way, Burk was critically engaging cultural phenomena. Bryan Dietrich is doing the same with *Prime Directive.* There is a fundamental difference between that pursuit and the heroic (and sometimes pornographic) fantasies found in fan-written fiction littered across the Internet.

Both Dietrich and Burk are not innovative in this regard. Poets and fiction writers have long engaged popular culture across the centuries. How many works have first taken their cue from Homer and the Greeks? Keats once famously ruminated on Chapman's translation of *The Iliad.* Where would Shakespeare be without Greek myth, Roman literature, and Holinshed's *Chronicle*? How many poets, had Shakespeare not existed, would have starved from a lack of material? Could Rainer Maria Rilke have become an icon of German literature, without having Orpheus to kick around? What about Virgil, in *The Divine Comedy*, leading Dante through the Inferno? And, let us not forget that Dante spurned the 'erudite' Latin to write in vernacular Italian.

There is one immediate answer. Those works are engaging in a long active neo-classical tradition – people who furiously type out, and then post online, their lurid James T. Kirk or Harry Potter fetishes are not. Yet, to smear Dietrich with the word 'fetish' does him a disservice. Fan fiction, at its worse, serves no purpose but to titillate the fan-writer's imagination. Dietrich, on the other hand, constantly seeks to *apply* pop cultural cues. James T. Kirk, under Dietrich's usage, becomes a tool to examine greater questions of life, society, and imagination. Neo-classical works, whether it's resurrecting Orpheus for the umpteenth time or dusting off the old Faust/Faustus legend, do exactly the same.

There are times when certain myths and legends lose their potency with a mass audience. Worse than that, they also can lose the cultural relevancy. If you were to randomly stop people on the streets of New York City, Chicago, Houston, Atlanta, and Los Angeles, a good number of them may not likely know Orpheus, Agamemnon, King Lear, or even Hamlet. But Homer J. Simpson? Not only would most know him, they could compare themselves, or somebody they know, to his dysfunctional antics, lack of prowess with power tools, and ability to say the most insensitive things at the wrong time. This isn't a failure of education, either. Rather, it is more of Homer Simpson becoming a metaphor more relevant to contemporary life. Dietrich is doing the same – he both appropriates James T. Kirk as a metaphor and a tool, but he's also able to step back and comment on that appropriation. He can contextualize, and in the process, he probes for an inner meaning.

Poetry would be nothing without metaphor. Writing poetry successfully is also a constant search for newer and fresher metaphors. For this reason, you can open practically any contemporary poetry journal and find enterprising new ways of appropriating language from both scientific and vernacular sources. It touches on something the Pulitzer Prize winning essayist John McPhee once noted, when asked about how and why he writes non-fiction. Geography, to paraphrase, is such ripe territory for metaphor. For Dietrich, 20th Century popular culture is that *ripe territory*.

Dietrich's poetic career has constantly sought to appropriate popular culture, examine it, and repurpose it as metaphor. His first book was *Krypton Nights*, a collection of poems about Superman and his supporting cast of characters. This work not only got Dietrich Neil Gaiman's blurbing attention, but uncommonly positive reviews across the poetic spectrum. The book itself won a Paris Review Prize. Unfortunately, *Krypton Nights* went—prematurely—into out-of-print-oblivion. Dietrich's second book, *Universal Monsters,* gave the same treatment to classic Universal Studios creatures. 2010 saw the publication of Dietrich's chapbook, *Love Craft* – and when it comes to the *Necronomicon,* Cthulhu, The King in Yellow, and others, I can't think of another contemporary myth-set that has passed through as many writers' pens, typewriters, and word processors. Now, *Prime Directive* continues the investigation.

There is more to come. Bryan Dietrich continues to write books, but there is more to it. In a way, he is the advance harbinger of what is to come. The 20th Century is now safely in the history books. It was a complex century, filled with both genocidal horror and wondrous imagination. That hundred years witnessed death and innovation on a scale humanity has never seen before. It will be scrutinized and studied for centuries to come. Sure, historians, scholars, and linguists will be at the forefront, but so will writers, artists, musicians, and poets.

Rich Ristow
Editor, (former) *Needfire Poetry*

Original Publisher's Note

Where No Man Has Gone Before

In late 2000, my grandmother was diagnosed with Alzheimer's Disease. Gran took the news rather badly at first, leading to temper tantrums, long phone calls to me with tears on both sides, and finally acceptance.

Over the next year, she tried hard to keep doing what she'd always done, but the tasks got harder and her memories slipped farther and farther behind. The woman who had once shown me how to relax my hand so I could separate my fingers into the Vulcan greeting, that same one who let me use pant-hangers as phasers, clothes hampers as shuttles and couch cushions as transporters, was gone. It wasn't long before she had to be moved to a nursing home an hour away from all of us, breaking her heart briefly—while she could still remember—and leaving my grandfather alone for the first time in over fifty years.

I knew better, but that didn't stop me from feeling like I had actually disintegrated her with one of those phaser blasts.

Gran died of complications due to Alzheimer's Disease in 2004, having outlived my grandfather by just eleven months. He himself had been diagnosed with a form of dementia not long after Gran was taken away, and I'll always think it was more a broken heart than anything else....

Bryan's poetry has put my grandparents, specifically Gran, back on that couch cushion, transporting her from 1980 to the present. Reading *Prime Directive*, I remembered all of my childhood with her, and how she shared my obsession with *Star Trek*, despite not understanding a moment of it.

Being able to publish such an epic homage has been humbling, and my eternal gratitude is forever in Bryan's hands.

Jodi Lee
Original Publisher, *Belfire Press*

It's five-year mission: to explore strange, new
worlds, to seek out new life and new civilizations,
to boldly go where no man has gone before.
                    —James T. Kirk, *Star Trek*

The road there, if you'll let a guide direct you
Who only has at heart your getting lost,
May seem as if it should have been a quarry....
                    —Robert Frost, 'Directive'

I.

Who misses ten? Two
tandem five-year missions in
and still no command?

Who recalls their prime
directive, that age, all that
awe? It's like the box

Spock opened in *Star*
Trek, the Medusa within
that made him mad, too

alien to touch.
And since ten? Even the stars
have moved, if only

just. Walk out tonight,
look up and find Orion.
Isn't his blue belt

a bit off? Aren't we
disturbed how much the sky has
shifted since we saw

through more earnest eyes?
We move as Earth moves, swinging
our slow circles through

even slower space,
our flesh flush with tectonics,
our minds alight, red

shifted, turning arcs
across all we call current.
Yet we do not move,

not really, not when
we consider, as we must,
the galaxial

hub, that vast ballast
between ourselves and the eye
of our gathering

star storm. Riding glass,
hurricanes of noble gas,
hydrogen, old gold,

we are taken up
into the storied middle
of things, move outward

from a center no
one—not Einstein, not Hopkins,
not Hawking—believes

we need to explain
how far we've come, how little
we are truly moved.

Eppur si muove.
They say Galileo said
this under his breath

when God's shock troops came
to take him away. And yet,
yes, we move. Chronos

eats his young, the stars
eat their own stones, the standing
dolmens dot the field

then wear away. Age
comes. Two old folk, a couple,
Greek, watch body parts

ebb out with the tide,
then, hearing some voice inside,
begin to toss rocks

behind them, begin
to build another race. Stone
on stone we stand here

like golems without
our maker. The sign we came
with, what has long since

washed clean from our brows
would only weight us down. Words...
we say them, we pile

them between ourselves
and the sky, we make up tales
to explain the way

we lost them, the way
we found so few in the first
place. We imagine

towers, whole peoples
surging over savannah,
becoming the stones

they couldn't speak to,
the cities they would not say.
We mark each passing

the way poor Hansel
did, after the bread, after
the blue herons came.

We leave words behind,
stones, pretending they'll be still.
But even our graves,

our tottering tombs,
too like the tumbling rocks
they can't recover,

move with the wayward
waves that call us down. We speak,
we give names, whisper

against the dark, yet
sound, even sound, even what
we saw and then gave

voice to, even light,
what lets us see, moves toward
that moment when it

wasn't. We are not
growing old. We are growing
into. Gravity.

As we fall apart—
we planets, we plots, we star-
stuff stuffed skin—we fall

together, slow, glow
brighter. Form from formlessness,
mutter made matter

II.

So, ten. What would you
give to be back where the rocks
started to pile up,

where the urge to pitch,
catch, suffer, recover them
began? No matter

the rough sand that seemed
to build, always, in pocket
bottoms; you carried

them the way *real* sky
scavengers might. A fragment
of moonlight, pyrite,

the fire-fused u-joint
of some Vulcan craft. They were
everything. Dander

of dreams, detritus
of deliverance. Rocky
reminders of all

you couldn't collect.
Pluto, Planet X, Quasar
3C212.

If you had blown up
then—your skin and skull so new,
unaccustomed to

all with which it pulsed,
convulsed—if someone had come,
sack in hand to claim

what remained, you, your
rock box would have been the same,
each vein rich with *or*.

Spiral notebooks scored
to the spine with black and blue
starships. Walls crawling

with X and Y-Wings.
2001's techno-sperm,
the *Discovery*.

The poor, doomed *Valley
Forge* suppurating with spoiled
arboretums. Moon-

scapes alive with Hawks
and Eagles, futuristic
cargo cults hauling

radioactive
landfill. The *Galileo*
7. Khan's coffin,

the *Botany Bay*.
NCC-170....
What? 1? Yes, but A

or B? It depends
on who counts. The *Nostromo*.
Not Conrad's of course,

but *Alien*'s. More
gore, more ore, all the artist
H. R. Giger cribbed

from Böcklin's 'Island
of the Dead.' So many ships.
Some stellar, others

earthly. Each dry-docked
in your room, ramped for release
from this island earth.

A whole habitat
of boy bait. Buoy-breasted
alien women,

Barsoomian broad
sides cuddling clouds, pillows,
Andromeda's ribbed

rock. Sword swaggering
human heroes. Helm-headed
Neros fiddling

among that dire, if
requisite, Rigelian
technology, green

buttons blinking out
of sequence, maniacal
laughter while worlds burn.

Miniature moon
bases, more rocks to make them
real. Dioramas

dreamed up from plastic
people, tiny tin hammers
ringing down on each

dead dilithium
drive, Death Star kill core, die-cast,
deep-space catafalque.

Always explosive
expectations, the end run
rationale, doomsday

detente. And every
night: dreaded dreams. Phaethon's
forbidden flight, Han

Solo's carbonite
casket, the fate of Kirk's crew,
episode 50,

'By Any Other
Name'…. Poof. Dodecahedrons.
All of this? War wounds

of wanting so much
more than, say, Oklahoma.
Give me a lever,

a rock to stand on,
oh, give me another world,
and I…you…could move.

'Give me a tall ship."
"Straight on to morning." "My God,
it's full of stars." Each

ship, story, stone…. Arks,
reeds, prayer beads. Ways to leave this
red, red rock behind.

III.

So what would I give
to love *Star Trek* again? Not
the new rehash, that

postmodern mish-mash,
but the stone cold kitsch of Bones
and Spock, that angry

erection called Kirk.
What it means to me now, well....
Nostalgia isn't

enough. Once I was
spellbound, struck by the simple
hubris of it all.

Every afternoon,
psyched, approaching our Zenith,
I'd flick the ON switch

and bathe in bathos,
wash myself clean in the light
that had to travel

through sky I wanted
so desperately to be
free from. Each dousing

was full submersion,
the old world rolling away
like a stone. *Buried*

in the likeness of
his death, raised in the likeness
of resurrection.

James Kirk. J. K., not
J. C., I know, but it's not
like he could discern

the difference. No,
where Kirk led, his crew followed,
and he expected

nothing less. Except
for a few expendable
red-shirts here and there—

the one or two who
beamed down into lava floes,
got shot by zeroes—

save these, Kirk saved them
all, often whole cities, worlds
caught in the balance.

How many cultures
could say, there but for the grace
of Kirk go I? How

many green women
walked away dressed, unimpressed?
How many saviors

seeded among stars?
No one was immune, not me,
not Federation.

Kirk had only one
rule, really. Other than that
odd prohibition

regarding Talos
IV (something like forbidden
fruit), Kirk's singular

directive, his prime
precept was the same as some
doctors': Do no harm.

And yet, well, I don't
remember one installment
where the apple was

withheld, where 'The Kirk'
allowed a graven image
before him. If 'Prime

Directive' means not
contaminating culture,
polluting the pure,

this singular five
year mission went belly up
long before lift-off.

Take 'The Apple,' or
'The Return of the Archons,'
perhaps 'Paradise

Syndrome, The' …. Any
one of them would suggest we
humans always know

best, computers, while
helpful, should not be our god,
and no matter what,

mystery is not
meant for forever. Who mourns
for Adonis? Kirk?

Never. Me? No. I,
like a good godless heathen,
would have pulled the same

wires were the machine
not right there in front of me.
Phosphordot pulpit,

front row pew.... *Not I,*
Lord, not I. I worshipped thus
at the foot of that

primal paradox:
Machines will take us away,
technology can

save us, propel us
past our years, but the human,
what we do with thumbs,

with stone knives and bear
skins...that's what truly moves us.
No external force,

no clockmaker, no
ultimate analog, no
adroit android should

own us, our future.
But what, then, was I watching?
Why did I adore?

IV.

Kirk's cock seemed to mean
more than even his phaser
might suggest. His gift

for overacting,
Bones' emotional outbursts,
Uhura's exposed

thigh, Sulu's sweaty
chest, Chekhov's illness, illness,
illness.... We should give

these, not some corny
cloaked craft, our rapt attention.
It's the human side

of that cardboard bridge
I guess I still remember.
Scotty's reels revealed

more than tricorders
ever did. And if Captain
Kirk had to kill God,

again, well then, his
onus only offended
the moneychangers,

only sent us back
to the temple, back to tear
down what cloth was left

between the holy
and that which we were meant to
be. Putting away

wives, husbands, childish
things—all nets, crooks, tax brackets
even—we, I, this

whole nation followed
a single enterprise, turned
to myth, to fable,

became Kirk's crew, cast
away between one orbit
and the next, between

one final frontier
and, well, the undiscovered
country. In the midst

of stones we chose our
captain, my captain, we chose
concentric circles

of sand and solar
sea, we chose our family
tree, our bodhi, our

last hour, erect ash,
olive bole carved to bedstead,
Ishtar's Easter ache,

Inanna's sole stake,
Shiva's lingam, some carney
carpenter's deadwood.

Chose an upright blade,
the journeywork of the stars,
a man headed home,

home to Ithaca,
home to the world, and let him—
Kirk, Kirké, Koan—

lead us, lose us, set
us spinning. How does one stand
behind the sound of

a bell? Where, Shangri
La? Satori? We followed
him, became fishers

of Zen. Then again,
Kirk was not your average
avatar. Modern

monk? Not on your life.
We saw him, granted, in robes,
but out of them more

often, in bed, red
in the face, apoplectic
with righteous fury.

So how a savior?
How, the pathos path reserved
for, say, Parvati?

Was it reflectors,
the cinematic stand-ins
for smoke and mirrors,

all those overdone
close-ups on eyes made maudlin
by gelled fresnel shine?

Or was it the fact
we knew how he was fractured,
saw it long before

his final hour?
We didn't need "Turnabout
Intruder" to tell

us what episode
five (what *every* epistle)
preached. The enemy

is within. Whether
we ditch our demons with stones,
bones, or neutral zones,

admit or forget
our ape amble, each hero,
David to Dalai

Lama, is never
only one. Kirk? Trinity:
leader, doctor, first

officer. All three,
flesh of his flesh, mind of his
mind. It, me, over

me. Freud, CG, both
would be proud. Consider, if
you will, Spock. Perhaps

he, more than James T.,
taught me the art of parting
sediment from sea.

V.

Imagine being
green only on the inside,
human on the out.

It couldn't have been
easy, forever the half
blood voice of reason,

the half that never
saw a yellow sun without
turning a bit blue.

Unlike the others—
Earther, Gorn, Grup, Romulan
even, those craven

kin—caught between blood
and blood, between competing
hues of hubris…. No

like, dislike, unsure
which road his humours, roving,
roamed, he'd never be

all his father ached
for, all his mother dreamed him
into. *Enterprise.*

What strange profession
for he who had no desire
to call home. Still, Spock

wanted out. Of this
I'm sure. Wanted as little
of reason as he

did of riot. One
world meant sustenance, yes, but
also stagnation.

The other, that vast,
batrachian underworld
of old emotion....

Well, one meant absence
of trees, of knees to hang by,
an absence of love

to tease or, better,
lose. The next? Otherwise. Whole
oratorios

of passions he found
so specious, so delicious,
so decidedly

damned. But then I say
wanted.... Spock *wanted* neither,
wanted both. I think

about this now, would
like to believe I wondered
even then: Is *want*

the same as desire?
Was he (are we, am I), is
*any*one able

to truly want what
they do not have, desire that
which they've never known?

Mr. Spock couldn't
have wanted anything. Least
ways not his Vulcan

half. And me? At ten?
Did I understand this? Fourth
grade, Oklahoma,

first generation
scholar? What precisely did
I recognize there,

in that green blood, Tau
Cetian ears? I recall
finding one Hallow's

Eve an unclaimed ream
of green posterboard, so green
I simply *had* to

make it bleed beneath
the faucet. It took three days
for that makeshift stain

to leave me human
again. But then I wasn't
forced to hide myself

under something felt—
billycock, cap, fedora.
No, I tried my dad's

uniform on once
or twice, his Colonel's colors,
scrambled eggs and all,

but it was always
too big for me. *He* was big,
bigger for the not

having been there. No.
Even when he wasn't off
on drills, he brought them

back for us. *Line up,
present arms. Have you policed
all your gear? Here…swabbed*

all decks? Prepped the P
X? Ready to storm the sheets?
Sir, yes sir, and then

bed. I didn't want
this, this or his later love,
mathematics, the square

root of a life laid
out by number. Years after,
in civvies, he still

dreamed in cadet, spoke
service. All parceled out, planned.
No passengers, just

pilot. Yet he loved
us his own way. And I guess
we loved him too. This

captain, this tall ship,
our millstone, our star. I was
far too green to know.

VI.

Logic, abandon….
Which way do we choose to live?
Spock found a middle

ground between the fixed
crystalline spheres of father
and that quarky Kirk.

Ptolemy/Bruno?
Spock/Kirk? It depends which side
of the slash you're on.

My sisters and I
are still infused with the blood
of our father, cursed,

blessed with his logic.
We had no Sarek, no, nor
Surak. Neither had

we Noonien Singh
or Kodos the conscienceless
king. But we did have,

still have, will always
be Daddy. My wife says we
are haunted by him.

Sometimes I agree,
but when my new son, ten now,
forgets to fold, say,

the hand towels lengthwise;
when he backs up the toilet
or knots the blind cord;

when he surrenders
half way up the hill, sled fled,
trembling, crying, cold

and beating baffled
snow furies into the earth
with frustrated fists;

when, among the wealth
of ages—bikes, books, mutant
robots I never

dreamed…. When he, like Spock
with a beard, like some mirror
world Lazarus, says,

"I hate my life"; when
he, unlike me, my sisters,
continues to live

his life without fear,
it's then I thank that Vulcan
blood, the human too,

and hold him until
my father goes away. It's
not like I don't know

he's there—I feel him,
his rage, the urge to act out,
be right. There are times

I forget to laugh,
when I feel torn between him
and me, between two

incarnations, two
minds. Matter, antimatter.
What I would give, those

days, for just a dime
of dilithium, Scotty's
Scottish vim, a bit

of Bones' bravado.
At Nick's age, I was alone,
in love with the stars,

with everything
I thought my dad would never
understand. He was,

still is, lost, staid, sold,
cuckold to a memory
he'd given up long

before I came. Wife?
Renting a room. Life? Same. Was
he ever pilot?

Did he really once
watch as something more than swamp
gas approached his plane

over Bermuda?
Can this be the same man who
drove from Carnegie,

OK, to L.A.
in under twenty hours, trails
of tickets littered

along the way? Is
this old man the man who reads
Star Trek by the pound,

or he who believes
Darwin's a dolt, that God put
big bones in the ground

just to test our faith?
He has nothing now, no one,
only an ex who

hates her needs, four kids
who beat back his anger when
it feeds, who would do

anything to buy
back all he's spent for just one
scent of pride. Just once,

when we all come back
for Christmas, it would be nice
to not speak Daddy,

to not let the talk
turn toward his faults like rocks
spinning, spiraling

in toward some star.
White holes, singularities—
all anomalies

that tear the fabric
of time. But what time is there?
What do we have left?

VII.

He may be dying.
Alzheimer's, dementia.
Small strokes, my mother

says. Everything I
remember makes me sad. How
he'd add big numbers

in his head while we
held up flashcards, how he turned
our bankruptcy round,

the offer he got
for TV weatherman or
that computer start

up. Yet none of it
materialized. No beam
out in the last scene.

No, instead, all his
yesterdays, all that naked
now, encased in air-

base basements. Tinker,
longest windowless structure
in the world. Over

a mile long. Enough
rock and grot to repot two,
maybe three Ramses.

Watching him wander
from hall to den, back to hall,
I imagine him

pacing those old stones
of his old job like Rilke's
panther. More...like he

paces the chambers
of his brain, looking for one
last shred of reason,

all that's no longer
buried there. His brain. At least
part of that remains

in me. Okay, not
the numbers—the best I can
do is guess prices

at the store before
they ring my groceries up.
A dubious gift

at best. But I see
patterns, am able to weave
in and out of texts

like a damsel fly
on crack. How much of what makes
me *me* is really

him? Are numbers so
different from words, programs
so far from far-flung

imagination?
One could label him concrete,
say his stone is more

Vulcan than Earth-born,
but then, these days, as he goes
slowly away, leaves

me with his four or
five hundred *Star Trek* novels,
as I listen, once

again, to the same
story for the four or five
hundredth time, mourn him,

his loss of nouns ("That
thing at the thing when we did
that thing.... Remember?"),

as he grows ever
more and more indistinct, each
day melting the way

his face has, the way
his memory has, the way
even his anger

has.... As I watch him
dissolve, beaming out his best
(even his worst) parts

to some strange new world
only he must recognize,
materializ-

ing one memory,
one noun, one fit at a time....
As I consider

him still half here, half
elsewhere, like Lazarus in
'The Alternative

Factor,' consider
him halved, only half human,
half sane, consider

the stark agony
of being at one's own throat
for the rest of what

must be, at its least,
eternity…. As I watch
his eyes dim, my own

face fading there, there,
even as it's transported
here, into something

so very like his,
I see he's begun to look
like Kirk or Kirk like

him and watch as he
struggles with all that *was* Kirk,
with all that has been

spent in him, all that
must spend in the space between
two universes.

Like Kirk, at last I
ask, "What of Lazarus? And
what of Lazarus?"

VIII.

Is he coming back?
Has he left yet? Are we all
eternal only

by virtue of this
protean procreative
habit? Is heaven

merely a good fuck?
Twain imagined us, after,
as horrible lyres,

as sucky Psalters
and gave up on the whole damn
idea. We live,

we shit, we make up
shit, we die. Somewhere in there
I guess we have to

enter each other,
leave the seed of what space we
filled behind, but then

who believes any
of that's enough? Even kids.
We combine matter,

smash the smallest stones
of ourselves together, re-
convene, converted,

in the womb, the world's
most convenient collider,
and poof. Me again.

You again. My dad
again. Is this the choice? Egg
or Elysium?

Magic or carpet
crawler? When we bump uglies
against ourselves, bang

each other, explode
like tiny stars in our mad
rush to get our rocks

off, what flame, what faint
ghost of flame, what midnight dead
lights are left to trace

connections between
where we were and where we've gone?
Does our image, flash

burned on the bodies
of our young, soothe them, make them
long for another

shroud? I saw a man
once on a street in Dallas.
It looked like he was

headed toward me.
In fact, he was turned, walking
away. Shirtless, bald,

he had the image
of a man I once thought of
as savior tattooed

across his body
but only on the back. Rise,
I thought, rise and walk,

and he did, watching
me as he went, trapped in skin,
in human skin. Me,

I wouldn't want that.
I never have. But sometimes
I'd like to believe

I carry my dad
that way. Sometimes I'd like to
believe, well, I don't.

It depends on who
I am at the moment, who
I want to be.

Am I my father?
Am I my father's son? Nick,
my son, is he mine

or someone else's?
Is his shape the shape of that
same fire? When we watch

Star Trek together,
am I forcing him into
Roger Korby's mold,

that man machine in
episode ten? Why do I
invite the old ghosts?

I remember him,
my father, watching with me.
I remember me

watching him watching
Kirk. We spent so many hours,
weekdays, each Wednesday

night this way. Even
church came second. It wasn't
enough for either

of us. Our notion
of passion had grown larger
than any stale pew.

Do I mean for this
to be, again? Do I want
my son to become

another me? Did
my father? In the long dark,
in that space between

cavern and craven
wood, walks a man, the first man
and his son. They hold

a torch between them.
It's always been this way. Fire
passing from skin to

skin. Tracks leading from
outpost to outpost. One strange
new world at a time.

IX.

Though I was never
only Kirk, I was often
only alien.

Alone with my Big
Little novels, comic books
in bags, my plastic

imagination,
faux encyclopedias
of every monster

I'd seen in *The Night
Stalker*, between the covers
of *Vampirella*,

Famous Monsters, *Plop*,
that one issue of *Hustler*....
Alone with each new

horror, I came to
sci-fi honest. My father,
though, introduced me.

How many 'evil'
comics did he sneak in to
me, under my mom's

nose? Tales of haunted
harps, men made of glass and sand,
women turned traitor

or, worse, witch. Children
served as *hors d'oeuvres*, traded in
for furred familiars.

Peculiar potions,
occult notions, not so rare
reasons to give up

on god. How many
red horrors, sad explorers
left for dead on worlds

where no one has been
before? No god—none of his
trappings. Or, yes, God,

but in different
wrappings. A vast, amorphous,
squatting thing, ruling

over its ruin.
And me to squat there with it,
beside some spaceman

with no other choice
but to worship what little
he has. Did I want

more? Did he? That me
at ten, alone in the den
with Captain Comet,

Adam Strange, Dr.
Strange? It is (so sorry) strange
how Mother got it

right. And my father
too. One wanted to lock me
in, safe from all she

didn't understand,
the other, to open doors,
as many as I

could keep quiet. So
I did, I kept them hidden,
kept myself hidden,

stayed inside, mostly
only played inside, made up
worlds I could rule from

within. Those comics
took me, indeed, they took me
but only because

my mother left me
no place else to go. They took
me, *Star Trek* took me,

Shazam took me, *Space
1999* took me,
Famous Monsters took

me, saved me, restored
to me my soul, returned to
me a faith I know

even my father
wouldn't have wanted. All that
I escaped alone

to tell thee, all that
blasted vastness, I traded
in for another.

How many heroes
and harlots, star-struck starlets?
Brawny, bone-brained geek

bigots all spandexed,
slick and Speedoed, all slab-abbed
and credoed? Amongst

this dreck, there was one
tale about a soldier. Small,
blonde. Pretty even,

said the comic. Yet
heroic. I didn't get
it then, probably

don't remember it
right now, but I know he was
out of his depth, out

of his mind. Hated
war, people, loved reading, loved
flowers. He practiced

Zen. Owned a double
bladed, white samurai sword.
He was very good

with it. Left alone
on an island, he fought off
monsters, saved himself,

the whole world perhaps.
Perhaps. I always wondered
how much he mattered.

X.

Charlie X, Miri,
the rugrats of Triacus....
All adorable,

all Adonic, all
abandoned. The Companion,
Trelane, Nomad, M-

5, Nancy Crater,
the women of the Sigma
Draconis system....

Children like Moses,
Osiris, like the apple
of Elohim's eye

or Oedipus left
lame on the mountain, V-Ger,
young Yonadans, Gem....

So many stories
on *Star Trek* were the same. Some
child left to its own

devices, bereft
of parents, grown now into
something so much more

than human. Savior
after savior, messiah
after messiah.

Did I know then how
tales aren't told by the teller?
How it's the other

way 'round, every one
of us molded by stories
we might not even

know? But we do know
those stories' stories, their pulp
progeny, ancient

ontogeny. Take
Kal-El, Krypton's crippled son....
He had no super-

vision growing up,
no original guiding
light, only Martha,

only Jonathan.
Lesser lights to rule those nights
he must have wandered

outside, looked up, longed
for second comings other
than his own. How awed

he must have felt. Odd
too, alien, and not just
because he *was* one.

Odd because he felt
an awe nobody else seemed
to recognize, not

there, not then, not in
him, not in the sky. He could
have told them, could have

said the words, tried to
explain the trajectory
of his craft, of all

that myth he'd become
a part of, but there, in that
state not so much state

as something between
they wouldn't have heard, or, worse,
couldn't. No, even

Merlin said, "Be still.
For it is the doom of men
that they forget." Yes,

that's it. We mistake
Christ for Clark, Moses for Man
of Steel, forgetting,

misremembering
into myth itself. It is
our loss that lingers.

Forget the forest
and gain the gates of hell, lose
Hel, promote panic.

Pan died for this sin,
so too Pandora, and Puck.
Prometheus left

so little light, left
aught but rock, a broken chain.
But then behind him,

before him, stretching
out, ascending like an arc
carved from dark, an arch

achieving in stone—
our old bodies—new storeys.
Level on level.

Our mortality
to Tiamat, Tiamat
to Gaia to Pan

to leviathan
to accuser to simple
snake, snake to Satan,

Satan to Dante's
plight, Milton's delight, Shelley's
monster's light, from dark

to dark, wight to white,
from Abraham to Israel,
Ahab to *Trek's* own

Khan we fight the blight
of memory with symbol.
We fill the abyss

with all we fear. Stone,
bone, snake, spark. Tempters. Saviors.
Apollodorus.

Valentine Smith. Ark
to Clarke, bow man to Bowman.
Kirk. Charlie X. This

XI.

is the abyss, this
break. It's why we tell stories
like beads. This, our soul.

Mohammed to T.
E. Lawrence, Lawrence to Mu'ad
Dib. We are Pilgrims,

beginners, enders,
covenants, unbelievers,
and the tales we drag

behind us, what we
often shape as shadow, what
we need but do not

really remember....
In the long dark, nothing is
abandoned. We may

try, we may forget
for a time, filling the space
once reserved for Ra

with Adams' rays, may
return from the wreck empty
handed, unable

to speak to our own—
my students don't remember
Skywalker, can't place

the crucifixion—
and yes, today we cannot
be certain even

Bible-Thumpers know
what it is they thump (they told
Nick he didn't *need*

his for vacation
Bible school).... But I have faith,
not in the God Nick's

never heard preached, not
the one my parents pounded,
but in the Gods God

replaced, the God God
got on all those Goddesses,
the Goddesses God

only ever thought
he'd left behind. We try—all
of us try. We leave

the nest, leave parents,
our parents leave us, but Rocs
return to the land,

the island isn't
ever utterly empty.
We hang here, waiting,

not waiting, moving
on, but when we need them, need
something to fill that

space (boy left on Mt.
Carmel, news at eleven;
abandoned children

found on Triacus)
we do what we've always done,
do what I did. Ten,

reading comics, lost
in the latest *Trek*, waiting
for my mom to wake,

for my dad to come
home, for life to resume, I
made it up. I made

my own soul. Fragments,
we are only fragments. We
are, as Possum said,

shored against our own
ruins. And history? It
always starts the same:

a child left alone.
I remember inventing
the rapture one day,

so afraid my folks
wouldn't return. I recall
2001, apes,

the way they approached
that anomaly. Afraid,
awed. How they filled fear

with fear, filled that yaw
with something they could touch. I
read the comic too,

read to understand
all I thought I'd missed, read with
dread and delight Jack

Kirby's awful prose,
his equally awful art.
Awe. Full. We touch stones

to know, to become
like Gods. And the apes? David
Bowman? Both, the same.

In that obelisk,
in the space we fill with more
space, we stand between

darkness and darkness,
between art and everything
that's not. Same again.

At ten, I couldn't
have known this. Neither could Nick,
not now. But we tell

our tales anyway.
We say, "God's left." "He's coming
back." We say, "Mother's

never going to
leave." We say, "I want to watch
another one, please."

 "Just one more, just…", say,
"I know how to save my son,"
say, "Please, not alone."

XII.

"Hail, hail, fire and snow.
Call the angel. We will go.
Far away. Far to

see. Friendly angel,
come to me." So sang the tots
of Triacus. So

sang that boy who was
me. Angels. Armageddon.
Neither got me off

this bloody rock. I
wanted something to take me,
aliens to screw,

even God, even
that pristine Chapel would do.
I sang. Chains. No sea.

Pity me, pity
me. No. That's not what I've meant
at all. It's just that

I worry about
my son. Yeah, just what the world
needs…yet another

dear doomed dork like me.
No recess, reads inside. Sports?
Hates them. Thinks most jocks

are cocks. Okay, good
for him, but I know what this
will mean. Each dragon

he draws on notebooks
now will be two more to fuck
him up later. When

he tells others God
doesn't have a penis or,
and I quote, "must live

outside of space, time,
broadcasting through all of us
like radios".... When

he sings 'Ring of Fire'
in Gollum's gargle, signs up
for *D&D*, chess

club, or, sweet Jesus,
accordion.... Each time says,
"Live long and prosper,"

"These are not the droids
you're looking for," I want to
shake him, break him. No,

tell him green is good
and hold him till the Klingons
go away. Each thing

he loves now matters.
What he will learn to love won't.
Not so much. And it

can't come back, not like
it is for him now. His mom
found her diary

some years ago, showed
me how, *every* Saturday,
she'd written "Watched *Land*

of the Lost today,
can't wait till next week." Bought it
soon after, watched it

again. Suffering
cats. Can we have ever have been
that lost? But I loved

it too. Loved *Trek* too.
How bad does it have to be?
How magnificent?

Shit. How little do
we need to know for that bit
to be it, to be

everything? And what,
now, means more than just the least
best thing to me then?

Maybe it's maudlin,
and yes I love my life, but....
Is there anything

today that touches
me like 'City on the Edge
of Forever,' Bones

gone postal? Is there
one moment, one book, one print,
one single sex act

that moves me today
the way I sat rapt by Kirk's
bare-chested besting

of that beast, the Gorn,
in 'Arena?' And though it
made me live again

every time I saw
it, that episode, others,
though I wish I could

go back…. Then…I know
then I wouldn't believe this
me, now, wanting it.

Out. We always want
out, no matter on which side
of the fallen star

we stand. Does this mean
I leave my son the way I
was left, deranged, drugged

by all that ten terms
prime? Let him reconnoiter
the ruins, that gate

way, arched stone, alone?
Season one, the next to last
episode…. Bones could

have saved one Edith
Keeler. Kirk kept him from it,
guarding forever.

* * * *

XIII.

I guess I saw Bones
as best of that starstruck lot.
The last pessimist.

Okay, Chekov too,
but it was Bones, always Bones
who excavated

deeper, looked beyond
the immediate drama,
took in the bigger

picture. Though the screen
was small, McCoy's monologues
invariably

brought the others up
short. He was, in the long run,
the only doctor.

I imagined me,
often, in his shoes, dying
to diagnose, say

what had to be said.
"Daddy, you're a bastard," or
"why won't you let us

love you." And in my
head, always also, "He's dead,
Jim. He's dead." No, not

one whit of the world
I actually lived on
would let me express

what was needed. "Kirk,
you arrogant asswipe. Fuck
the girl—let's get off

this lousy planet."
"Spock, you intergalactic
hypocrite, just cry

and get it over
with." Captain, First Officer,
Father, frigging fool....

I watched him, Daddy,
pine for years, holding onto
what could not be held.

It's not like our years
alone, ten to twenty, were
without their stolen

moments. That damn show
itself was wonderful, I
admit. I never

would have known it sans
the sadist. But now, forty,
I suddenly know

how much I must mean
as he offloads those novels,
Star Trek all, to me.

He's re-reading them,
see, at the end, losing them,
one by one, even

before he lets me
take them. Forgetting, the best
he can, *into* me.

I'll be the only
one to remember. The last
doctor to give him

his diagnosis.
So I savor all those nights,
staying up, playing

221B
Baker Street or *Consulting*
Detective, recall

his shit-eating grin
even when—ever so less
than often—I'd win.

Was it pride, the hope
he'd made something at last last?
Or the way he drove

all over Memphis
for me, scoring the latest
lone issue of *World's*

Finest, the only
copy of *The Two Towers*
one could find. He taught

me to cook, to pay
bills, to read religiously,
how to wash, iron,

play penny poker,
how never to lose too much….
Called him the other

day. Asked him over.
Told him he should come see our
local aerospace

museum. Back when
he was a pilot, back when
he still had a chance

Bryan D. Dietrich

to be 'astronaut,'
not just 'desk jockey,' back when
he still had friends, one

was on Apollo
13. The *Odyssey*, I
said, was on display

here. *Bryan*, he said,
what's that? And I? Daddy, it's
the one that almost

didn't make it back.
Pause. *From where*? And then, after
I'd explained. *Bryan....*

Yes. *Did we ever
go to the moon?*...I have his
books now. Almost all

of them. I have Bones,
both bound and in my brain. Bones,
Bones saying, "He's dead...."

XIV.

James. Tiberius.
Scene-seizer, overactor.
It always comes back

to him. And William
Shatner too, I suppose. Born
1931,

same year, almost same
month as my dad. If McCoy
was the empath, what

does it say that he
was the first crewman to die?
The captain tried to

rescue them all, save
all of us, the world, maybe
me, a lot. But then

sometimes the savior
is deaf to the tale he's come
to tell. Remember

Arthur, remember
Merlin trying to explain
to him who he was,

how he came to be,
all he stood for…. Remember
how Arthur, his knights,

all those standing round
laughed at him, Merlin, the fool,
as he said, "Stand back!

Be silent! Be still…
and look upon this moment.
Savor it…for you

are joined by it. You
are one under the stars." Yes,
and not one of them

listened. Not Arthur,
not Kirk. Even my father,
well, he missed the point.

He didn't know how
to draw the sword from all that
stone. Yes, sometimes Kirk

used a blade. And yes,
fantasy is fantasy.
Swords swords. But the earth?

Earth is always hard.
When Mother first left, two years
before our sojourn

in Soulless City,
we moved to a flat across
from the regional

park. By now I'd turned
to fifth grade, begun getting
beaten up for real.

Every day, some new
boy beast. Not to overcome,
no. To pacify

at best on the long
way home through that park. Each time
the bell rang, I knew

I had the gauntlet
first, then the forest, and then,
only then, refuge.

Dar J. Falls. He fell
on me most often, forced me
to say I'd suck him

before he set me
free. And that wrestler who'd been
held back so many

times...once he made me
guess names of planes as they passed.
Flat on my back, his

cleat cleaving into
Adam's apple, I grappled
for what my dad had

told me, named each one,
all he'd ever flown. Just this
once I must have, well,

surprised him. *Bless me,*
Father. Unless you bless me,
I will not let you

go. And so I ran,
ran to that one place the park
provided for me.

I'd never seen one
before...nor since...but that park
had an *Enterprise.*

Probably not scale,
the proportions were enough
to make any least

geek laugh, but not me.
Here, said Boorman's Lancelot.
Here is my domain,

within this metal
skin. How many days did I
hold up there, waiting

in that irony
of ironmongery, how
many adventures

invented, monsters
mangled, beat back by those walls
of my father's dream?

When I was small, he
used to come home from duty,
let me root in his

flight suit pockets, take
his leftover Lifesavers.
Wasn't till we moved,

going though drawers, that
I found his stash. Green. Whole rolls.
All untouched for me.

XV.

These, the voyages
of the starship *Enterprise*.
These, the planets, rocks

they came to explore:
Excalbia, where the men
were *made* of rocks, swords

smelted by lava
spoor. Janus VI, another
creature from the core.

Delta Vega, where
no man had gone before, where
Gary Mitchell dug

Kirk's grave, carved a tomb
from lithium ore. Vulcan?
Here Spock's soul returned

to stone. How about
that planet roses were grown,
where Kelvans condensed

the crew to bouillon,
mineral, bone? Yonada?
Here denizens die,

not knowing their home
is hollow, that one has touched
the sky. Or Gamma

Trianguli VI....
God himself: big bricks. Maybe
Miramanee's world,

pagan paradise...
big rock coming, comet, ice.
The starship itself,

brown dwarf off the prow,
driven by dilithium
a stone's throw from now....

What was it Frost wrote?
"Never tell me that not one
star of all that slip

from heaven at night
and softly fall has been picked
up with stones to build

a wall." Yes, something
there is that loves loam, earth foam,
this thin skin only

six miles thick in spots.
We ride our rolling rock round,
unaware, mostly,

of the soil from which
we spring, the stolen star ooze
that lurched us to land.

In reaching out past
each next beach to next farther
shore, in finding what

waits beyond—planet
to planet, there, just behind
that rock—we rack up

walls. What takes us up,
then, up and out, every reach,
lets us know just how

short the span between
knuckles and the earth they drag.
Daddy, for instance,

spent one fall leaving
coin trails, bright breadcrumbs, throughout
our new bachelor flat.

Pennies first, nickels
next, and on toward some end.
Sometimes Tupperware,

bottomed up boxes,
bowls. And always three choices.
His stab at *The Price*

Is Right. Under one
tub, a single paperclip,
under the next, mint.

The last? Cash. That, or
a note, impromptu treasure
map. It was, I guess

his way of making
that path between one life lost
and one yet to lose

easier to track.
Day on day, I remember
following those coins,

breathless, curious,
but knowing with every step
we were one quarter

closer to bankrupt.
For each dime I diminished,
divorce had devoured

even more. We were
poor, not two good rocks to rub
together, but those

nights, tracking Dad's mad
money, mint minerals, were,
sorry, precious. Coin

to coin, hand over
and, ore to or, we spelunk
our way through this cursed

universe, spectral
spacefarers in search of new
seas, dice diviners,

rollers of bones, card
clairvoyants. In the Tarot,
sometimes protection

signs are pentacles,
sometimes coins, wealth to be leant....
But sometimes, sometimes

when all is spent, no
more saving left in the bones,
sometimes coins are stones.

XVI.

Daniel said a stone
would be thrown, kingdoms would fall.
Moses smote one. Lot's

wife became one. Christ
claimed they cried out. And Peter?
Peter was called rock.

Yeah, so was Rodan.
And the Abomination,
and Benjamin Grimm.

Quetzalcoatl
too. In the film *Forbidden
Planet*, Morbius

says, "You cannot look
on the face of the Gorgon
and live." Mr. Spock

found this out the hard
way. And Odysseus'
men, and Perseus,

and Isis's bro,
and even Shiva's penis.
How hard the rapture

makes us. The sublime.
When we look in the abyss—
Ahab sneaking peak

over longboat lip,
Percival perusing cup—
the image we see

Bryan D. Dietrich

is ultimately
always us. It's just that, well,
when I see my son,

he me, I want it
to be less minotaur, more
maze. Poor Theseus

had it right. He fought
that bad boy—half it, half man—
hand to hand. Wulfie

too. In the great Hall
of the Heart. Christian or not,
Jew or Jaian, we're

all the kin of Cain.
Marked. As stained by our own best
beast, as fucked, as Spock.

Just this past Christmas
we had what my mother calls
Dinner and a Show.

It started small, it
always does, something about
stockings, my sister

overstepping her
space. Unable to find those
we usually

used, she offered up
one she'd brought, an extra sock
to stuff chock-a-block

with crap. And Daddy,
Daddy overreacting,
flying toward his

habitual found
fury, came out swinging. Not
literally, not

at first, but among
the night's screaming, when I stood
up at last, found bones

enough in my spine
to stand against the spittle,
called him what Doctor

McCoy would have called
him, "You inconsiderate
fuck," I found myself

facing down all I'd
ever feared. It wasn't just
ghosts of bullies past,

all those prosaic
Khans, trails of tribulation,
humiliation,

awe, some whale-toothed yaw,
that black gap stretching back, back
to when I was bathed

in Baptist, brainwashed,
stainwashed, guilty and alone.
No, nor was it just

the father I feared
I might become. When he turned
on me, frail fists raised,

face convulsed, the kind
of rage I'd only ever
read about, I think—

Bryan D. Dietrich

that moment, forced to
take his hands in mine, to stand
eye to eye with it—

I think I saw what
we fear when we fear all that
fades away. There was

nothing of 'Father'
there, no fine shine, what we find
time to sign into

song—the reason for
flight, for light, all right, all wrong,
what Hyde realized, what

he cursed, civilized.
No, God gone, his myth stripped off,
he, it, he, the thing[1]

I faced was clean, our
primal dream of what we knew
before fire, before

we started stalking,
began talking, and, nothing
to say, slunk away.

[1]*A fact worth noting:
The Shape in Halloween wore
a Captain Kirk mask.*

XVII.

All of it's going
away. Everything we had.
The world as my dad.

The world as Captain
Kirk in 'Dagger of the Mind.'
Here, on Tantalus

V, Dr. Adams
tries to drain Kirk's brain, take his
mind from him. Had it

worked, had he unkirked
Kirk, what would've remained? Beast?
That thing, Christmas Eve,

I spent denying?
In 'The Deadly Years,' 'Return
to Tomorrow,' 'Spock's

Brain,' in each of these
episodes, some part of our
crew is deleted,

cut out, and the rest?
What do we have when we are
we no longer? When

Menelaus means
nothing, when Io isn't
even a moon, when

Merlin's crystal cave
and Arthur's Avalon are
forgotten? Our world

is awash in wave
after wave of distraction.
Faces of Death, Cops,

Fox, *Big Brother, Doom,*
reality T.V.... V.
D., ultimately,

of the brain. Others'
pain. What would've made Gandhi
blind. The mind whacking

off. Yes, we have deep
dish cable, can watch Cain kill
Abel, but do we

still know who they are?
Can we share stories, relive
glories we even

recognize? Since we
first climbed up from crud, earth's blood,
out of stones, earth's bones,

what we've told ourselves
is what we became. Now, long
past the age of steel,

deep in the eon
of ether, humanity
begins to forget.

Here, without our tales,
how do we identify
us, even *them*? No

Shakespeare to teach, no
Milton, no, nor his reach. God
forbid we grant Twain

any clemency.
Quixote? Too dead, uptight.
Invisible Man?

Too heady, white. Like
Bradbury in *451*:
Without offense, no

flame, we're underdone.
Too many channels, too few
to understand, too

much to remember,
not one—one—good man. Sodom,
Gomorrah—they're gone

as well, drowned in this
Letheian river. Aw, hell,
we have iPods, i

Phones, internet, Wii,
but move along, move along,
nothing to see, not

one thing that lingers,
nothing that stays. No *reason*
for rapture, just joy

sticks, T.V. trays. So,
what about *Star Trek*? The last
great myth? No one but

the freaky faithful
really gives a shit. We, like
my dad, watch it all

depart. Hero. God.
Savior. Soul. Art. And here we
sit, left behind, stones

without a story,
sand without sea. Stonehenge. Big
blue rocks. No rubric.

No key. The madmen
have taken the asylum,
like on Tantalus

or on Elba II,
like in *Arkham Asylum*
where only Jokers

would do, 'Benito
Cereno' perhaps, Melville's
switcheroo, or it

all goes back to Poe,
his craven, mistaken stars.
We're all Professor

Fethers, all little
Dr. Tarrs. Our inmates are
escaping, we join

them in the gym, but
none of us can recognize
which storey we're in.

XVIII.

Sometimes the preacher
still gets the best of me, that
hellfire fool I grew

up with. He took me
like *Battlestar* took me, like
he took my mother.

So, both of us, fucked.
All but my oldest sister
gave up, after that,

on God. I can't speak
for the rest, but know my dad
must have left the pew

when he couldn't live
with any more imagined
resurrections. Though

that ability,
the gift of filling in gaps…
it's this which makes us

what we are. It's what
drives us to explore the X,
the ex, the unknown,

from the abandoned
Exeter to Exo III,
from Excalbia

to *Excalibur*.
And though I mourn all those dead
Gods, I mourn Kirk too.

I know that comics,
Saturday corn, internet
porn, are all a part

of the problem, but
no one knows when the lectern
will turn, when the words,

say, Spock said, will be
glossed in red. No, wonder is
wonder. We are, each

of us, souls seeking
to cement our story. Each
of us, faltering

in the forest, seeks
what will rise, an enterprise
to make all the walls

familiar. Okay,
last tale. That same first summer
after our divorce,

I had invited
a friend over. No big deal
unless it'd not

happened before. Mom....
Before I went with my dad
she'd forbidden friends.

No sleepovers, no
birthday parties but one. Now,
it was all new, just

me and my father.
Freedom. My friend—let's call him
Paul—and I, we found

ourselves, less than dressed,
in the closet. There, I held
it in my hand, soft,

an alien egg
sac suspended from the crotch
of our closet cave.

His cock and my own,
alien too. Suddenly
stone. It wasn't real.

We didn't do much.
But the preacher doesn't care.
That voice in the dark

calls, *Where art thou? Who
told thee that thou wast naked?*
Asks, *Hast thou eaten....*

We were young yet, near
naked in our hunger to
know what feelings mean.

Awed, underwear down
our knees, we touched each other,
fumbled for something

which might surpass that
simple recognition: None
of this can last. Boys

do this, too afraid
not to seek their salvation
in the dark. I rode

bikes with my father
every day that season. See,
Paul's mom suspected

her son. Came knocking
more than once, and I didn't
want to be at home,

didn't want my dad
to know. Cycles. Tree tortured
avenues. We scratched

each one off some map
we'd yanked from an old *Yellow
Pages*. Summer. Still

my father's worship
word. I know that all I feared
brought us closer, but....

But. Like *Star Trek*, Zod,
God, like marriage, Merlin, what
isn't there, the knock

that never comes, it's
only as real as we let
it feel. Sometimes, this

is enough. Sometimes,
when my father remembers
us then, I let him.

XIX.

Someone said the old
fathers still pray for us there,
up on their mountain,

up amongst the stars,
up, not down, down, not up, caught
somewhere between us

and ether, Yahweh
and yaw, the *this* and abyss,
where all the crossroads

echo, are echoed
by cave, by the grave, by cairn,
by bone become stone,

by skull where it sticks,
cold Calvary's crucifix,
where the brain, Darwin's

drain, evolution's
orphan, stacked, animal-packed,
recalls itself, us,

abandoned by time,
each an ark on Ararat,
each an alien

stone thrown down to dirt
by other, farther rocks, Sol's
clocks, Mecca's black stone,

what Mohammed called
Alhajar Al-Aswad, this
or Assyria's

onyx obelisk,
Christ's cave cork, perhaps Barnum's
brittle giant or

a hieroglyphic
rose...after all, these rocks are
merely metaphors

for me, me and you,
our lives, our lingering lapse,
falling to feldspar

from the trees, picking
up stones, piling one on one,
ore on ore, digging

into the smallest
grottoes of things, cave-diving
for quarks, for strange, charm,

up, down, beauty, truth,
repacking everything to
take with us when we

leave all this behind,
when we understand at last
song in silicon,

marvel in mica,
quartz contentment, hematite
hermetics, basalt

bravado, the lack
of shame in shale or schism
in schist, but this, all

this is only ours
long after those bone-brawlers
already freed flint,

after their gypsum
jamboree, magnesium
magnificat, that

metamorph moment
when rock was rock no longer
but basis to build

Teotihuacán,
Sacsayhuaman, Machu
Picchu, Kailasa,

each Itza, Petra,
Djoser, Giza, every site
where we've carved ourselves

from karst and col, each
hanging Babylon, mountain
monastery, honed

horn, plateau plenty,
eternal escarpment meant
to stop time, image

the image of all
that is Buddha, say, Pablo
Neruda, all fine,

in geosyncline,
every holy mount, from Song
Shan to Wu Tai Shan,

Arunachala
to Ayer's Rock to Devil's
Tower, Mount Horeb

to that bier where we
began, Athos, away from
the things of man, or

all those henges, Stone,
Newgrange—megaliths, geo-
glyphs, the Nazca range—

or every wall, Floyd's
to China's, wailing, others,
dear Diana's, her

temples, her brother's,
that Delphi crack where sibyls
smoked, rocky remnants

of Mars attack, all
staring back up into black,
the clear we came from,

like Easter Island
gods, like my dad, head over
handle bars one Fall,

same spread-eagle as
that torn Titan on his slab,
so near my metal

mother, that spaced craft,
false raft, that wood, that sleep, that
bridge he failed to leap.

XX.

That was the first time
I saw my father fall. It
happens more often

now, if not so much
on stone. He says he has *his*
planned out, paid for. *Dry*

bones, dry bones…. What's left
of the fortune he never
had, tied up in tomb.

It's all he will leave
me, after his books. So what
wealth *do* we bequeath

our sons? *Hip bone, leg*
bone…the name of the Lord. Do
we hear it, whisper

it ourselves, do we
pick up? Is there anything
more than these dying

connections? That black
telephone Sylvia spoke
of, is it still off

at the root? Or do
roots remain, riddling us
like Victor's victims,

like my son, the mad
scientist experiment.
In-vitro. Sci-Fi

incarnate. His mom
tried to explain it to him
early on, using

Bryan D. Dietrich

green glass containers
like some lunatic Lady
Frankenstein. I can

just see her mixing
food coloring, opening
the sesame oil,

saying, "See, this is
the sperm donor's donation.
This, my own. Look how

the colors mix—blue
fluid, ochre oil—and this?
Here's the emerald

elixir of you."
And me? Ten years into this
equation, a free

radical, never
father till now, what have I
given, what part is

left for me to add?
After all I've seen   *When I
was a child, I caught*

a fleeting glimpse   all
my father wanted, all he
loved, my Mother, his,

the one who carried
him into that dark apple
out of the corner

of my eye. I   hold,
into that cellar, away
from the coming storm,

the one who   *turned to*
look but   loved him just enough
to lose the other

child she carried, that
and…   *it was gone. I cannot*
put my finger on

and, well, herself   *it*
now. The child is   all he had
to live with, mother

dead, father distant,
blaming…   *grown, the dream is gone…*
effectively gone.

Okay, I know. Such
melodrama. But this was
The Wall, the mood ring

I revolved inside
growing up. How many nights,
up late, did I spend

listening to that
album, imagining its
more mundane monsters,

speaking with the dead?
Telling them, telling myself,
"Do not be afraid

of him, do not be
terrified, do not be be-
wildered. Be joyful,

and recognize him
as the form of your own mind."
By then I'd long left

the Baptist behind,
found the eightfold path, Zen, made
my own garden, rock....

Enough. But what is
enough? And where do I find
answers? The *monsters*

of rock, Tibetan
Book of the Dead? And if not
these, if not my dear

nearly departed
father, who? Kirk? Spock? Bones? How
about General

Order #1,
the Prime Directive itself?
No fucking around

with the natural
'next' of things, the primitive,
no matter how well

meaning. My dad fucked
up, fucked *me* up, in order
to save me. I know

this now. He will die,
soon, tomorrow, a long time
ago, not so far

away, for all I
know, now, *just* now—my sister
calling while I write

this today, my son
finishing the last Potter,
that carpenter clone

like Kirk, like Arthur,
all the others—now, while I
recall the final

Trek, the last *real* reel,
seventh seal, *Generations*,
Kirk saving all those

suns, again, dying
again, on the bridge again,
going boldly, what

he'd only ever
dreamed, falling from a far less
boundless bridge to stone,

looking up into
the face of he who must come
after, another

captain's, my captain's,
my Colonel's eyes, seeing
him see me, himself

at last, now, seeing
that final episode now,
all nexus, new. Now

hearing our son say,
"Just one more, please. Don't go, I..."
And him? Jim? "Oh, my."

Bryan D. Dietrich

*At the other end of the transporter, you need to have some blob of
atoms that represents Captain Kirk but has no information in it. I
mean, what would that look like?*
  —Christopher Monroe, Joint Quantum Institute

Is there anybody out there?
  —Roger Waters, *The Wall*

Afterword
Star Trek as Myth

Captain James T. Kirk stands in the middle of a stone labyrinth deep beneath the surface of a strange planet, hiding from Ruk, an android intent on killing him in order to protect the plans of his newest master, Dr. Roger Korby. Five years past, Korby himself had his mind downloaded into an android body after losing most of his biological self to frostbite. This planet, Exo III, was once inhabited by Ruk's makers, a race of astonishing technological prowess. Using the Old Ones' technology, the mad doctor intends to transform Kirk and the crew of the Starship Enterprise into androids, to spread androidism across the galaxy, and to 'save' humanity from its biological shortcomings.

Korby has already 'replaced' Kirk; stripping him naked, forming a rudimentary golem out of clay, then strapping both figures into a oversized centrifuge where, after spinning like a deranged dreidel, two fully-formed Kirks appeared. Now that the captain's alter ego is up and running, Ruk searches for the 'unnecessary' original among the underground caves and corridors, calling out in a mimicked voice of Nurse Chapel. Kirk, lying in wait for this assassin intent on destroying his 'imperfection,' breaks off a stalactite from the ceiling and holds it in his hands. Aware of the fact that he is no match for his much larger stalker, Kirk needs a weapon to help defend his identity.

The stalactite he holds looks exactly like a giant penis.

When I first saw this episode of *Star Trek*, it was 1976. I was in fourth grade. I watched it with my father—sharecropper's son, cotton picker, child prodigy, Air Force colonel, jet pilot, Air National Guard transport pilot, Apollo program recruit, world class chess player and computer programmer. I watched it with a man who was teaching me what it meant to be a man. I also know that at age ten, I watched it with little or no awareness of the metaphors at work. The episode 'What Are Little Girls

Made Of?' (in fact pretty much every episode of that garish, garbled, grand, original series) might as well have been titled 'What Are Little Boys Made Of?' or 'What Is Identity?' Episode after episode asked this question.

From 'Mudd's Women,' 'The Enemy Within,' and 'The Man Trap' to 'The Naked Time,' 'Dagger of the Mind,' and 'The Conscience of the King'; from 'The Menagerie,' 'Arena,' and 'The Alternative Factor' to 'The Return of the Archons,' 'Space Seed,' and 'This Side of Paradise,' well over half of just the *first* season's storylines address questions of self—questions of who we are in the face of technology and time, reason and religion, genetics and gender, light years and love. When Kirk is forced to save the future by letting Edith Keeler die in Harlan Ellison's masterpiece 'The City on the Edge of Forever,' the primary characters learn the same lesson they will have to struggle with years later in *The Wrath of Kahn*: the needs of the many outweigh the needs of the few. As he has to do many, many times in the series, Kirk gives up love for larger principles, he gives in to the inevitable. But he also fights, he also weeps.

Much has been made of Kirk's dalliances, his predisposition toward shirtlessness and shagging. Great sport has been had over William Shatner's nearly infinite capacity for overacting, but the series seems to understand that this particular starship captain is not so much individual as archetype. He stands more for ideas than for any misguided attempt at mimesis. I am certain I did not know this at ten, but I am just as certain that I did. Kirk became a fictional avatar, a simplified simulacrum of my father, of me, of what I needed to know to become what I've become. Of course there was also Spock and Bones, but Kirk was the focus of the show and the center of my universe. The alien and the doctor served as stabilizing forces for the central ego of the epic, yes, but Kirk was what I wanted to evolve into, what my father already seemed to be.

Obviously, I was too young to 'know' such things, to recognize the elements of the extended metaphor evident in many episodes, particularly the one described above. But the thing about archetype and symbol is that it works on the subconscious level. It is all *about* the subconscious level. It *creates* the subconscious and thus the consciousness that later overlays it. Take the above scene: Kirk (the self), fighting to maintain his integrity (actualization), wanders the underground catacombs (the unconscious) and is stalked by an exaggeratedly masculine construct (animus) while it speaks in a feminine voice (anima) in order to ensure Kirk remains only machine (reification). The whole episode is steeped in issues of humanity versus homogeneity—new versus old, reason versus instinct, flesh versus spirit, etcetera. Further, the episode's writer, Robert Bloch, named the ancient race the 'Old Ones' in homage to H. P. Lovecraft, another writer deeply interested in the nature of self and Other. Ruk is even played by Ted Cassidy, an actor best known as another 'made' man: Lurch, from *The Addams Family*.

Are we a simple aggregate of experience? Can we be downloaded? What sort of fidelity would be lost in a copy of ourselves? Should we fight to maintain the solidity we see in our own minds, in our children's? What *are* we fighting? Masculinity, femininity, stone, silicone, the Old Ones we have reason to fear? These are the questions a single episode of *Star Trek* imprinted on me, on my subconscious, on the rudimentary clay-like form of my early psyche. These are the same questions I could ask about my father and me, about myself and my son.

Watching this show with me, my father was the Old One and I was his golem. As it turns out, I did not wind up with a complete imprint of the man (either his or Shatner's), but a huge portion of what I am today is indeed based on his engrams, his likes, his passions for, say, science fiction and story, melancholy and mystery. My father was a math genius, a military man, an angry man. I am a poet, a scholar, and (I hope) a man of peace. But whether I note the similarity of our taste in entertainment, our desire to work with great focus on ever smaller and smaller parcels of meaning (numbers or nouns), whether I recognize a similar tendency toward egomania or frustration with multitasking, I must admit, like so many of Lovecraft's characters or *Star Trek*'s themes, I cannot escape the Old Ones... the guilt of Kodos or the superiority complex of Kahn, the dreams of Captain Pike or the judgment of the Metrons. Like Professor Robert Crater—like my father—I have lingered too long over lost love. Like an infected Spock—like my father—I have fought the primordial, naked urges that erupt from time to time. Like the followers of Landru—like my father—I have fallen prey to reductive and destructive mythologies. I am and always have been 'of the body.'

This might suggest only the negative. I learned far more positive things from *Star Trek*, from Kirk, from his crew, from my father in all his forms. I learned how to make sure the bills are paid even if the money doesn't seem to be there. I learned how to love someone beyond all reason, how to change sparkplugs, play chess, read good books, how to collect comics and do algebra, how to ride a bike, take a punch, suck it up. I learned family first. I learned how to cook and clean and be patient, how to listen, how to tell a story. I learned how engines work and computers and planets. I learned how to love education, how to revere it, how to study and how to write. And while all of these things are important, I also learned—and learned well—how *not* to do just as much, how not to love, not to teach, not to let the bills or the anger or the insignificant pile up, how to try and keep my father's shortcomings from becoming my own.

Finally, I learned that life, that self, must be a balance. One could point out (and many have) that the three primary characters of the show represent several possible triune models of the mind, of self, of world view. One could observe how the characters attempt, always, to find balance between these perspectives, these alternately agonistic and complementary paradigms:

Kirk = Courage
Bones = Heart
Spock = Brain

Kirk=Ethos
Bones=Pathos
Spock=Logos

Kirk=Father
Bones=Holy Ghost
Spock=Son

Kirk=Id
Bones=Ego

Spock=Superego

Kirk=Shadow
Bones=Anima
Spock=Animus

Kirk=Reptilian Complex
Bones=Limbic System
Spock=Neo-cortex

And while any one of these models would apply, suggesting several viable visions of the show's message, as well as several practical paradigms for how the self can be divided, I prefer the following breakdown:

Kirk = Instinct
Bones = Empathy
Spock = Intellect

This is how a man should be. These are his parts. I learned a lot from my father, mostly his Kirk part and his Spock part. I learned how to evade the enemy approaching in the labyrinth and how to knock him senseless. I learned instinct and intellect, how to find and wield the club of what passed for masculinity in the Seventies. It's big and it swings. What I *didn't* learn from my father or these two avatars, I learned from my sisters: empathy. While my father was off on trips, flying across continents, going where many men had gone before, I wandered the byways of other underworlds, the land of Woman, the grotto of the secret sharer. I learned from my sisters, who also loved *Star Trek*. I learned, like Bones' character so amply exemplifies, that one can be empathetic and still be masculine. That masculine doesn't really mean much at all. That one doesn't have to be armed with a penis to fight, to feel, to fully realize the power of that which heals. What is *in* the body is as important as what hangs upon it. After all, it isn't Kirk's martial prowess that gets him much of anywhere. Often it's his intellect, as in 'Arena,' but just as often, maybe *most* often, it's empathy. What holds up the flesh and the brain, the primal and the prescient? What scaffolds our souls? Bones. Always bones.

Bryan D. Dietrich

Alas, such lessons didn't protect my body. They may have fed my sense of self and provided a philosophy that served me well into my first half century on this planet, but empathy only made the bullies worse. At least at the time. Shortly after watching all those episodes of *Star Trek* with my father, my parents found themselves divorced, and I found *myself* living with my father in a strange new world, a new civilization of alien boys who, like the denizens of the episode 'Spock's Brain,' saw me *not* as a brain, not as 'Morg,' but as 'Eymorg.' Fifth and sixth grade were hard. Lots of bullies. Lots of alienation. Expected, I suppose, for a poet. But I did have one safe haven on the way home from Steed Elementary. To get to our bachelor apartment, I had to walk through a park. In that park—away from the other boys who seemed to be all instinct, no intellect, even less empathy—I found a piece of playground equipment that became a better escape than any science fiction. Regional Park came equipped with a large metal replica of the Starship Enterprise.

In the same way my father and my sisters and some silly TV show had helped form the shell of the self I found myself inhabiting, this *real* shell served as a place to hide, a place to re-imagine myself, to become the Kirk I wanted to be. For a time, I believed it protected me…from bullies, from my father's angry eruptions, from my own insecurities, from the divorce that had left us both lost in space. It allowed me to imagine all sorts of alternative realities; put me, literally, in the driver's seat of that ship. One vessel inside another. What was inner became outer. And I soared.

Of course, the Enterprise wasn't what I wanted. It wasn't any more real than Kirk or Kahn or Klingons. I still clung to an ideal, still unaware that the ideal was only an underpinning for what had to come later. Like the Prime Directive itself, the lessons of *Star Trek* weren't meant to replace action, but give focus and meaning *to* action, to provide star charts for the journey ahead. Little did I know that what lay before me, eventually, would be my father's losing battle with identity.

For years, I have treasured my memories of *Star Trek*. I have collected the entire series, watched it with my own son, discussed it, written about it, memorized most of it. I keep a phaser and a communicator and a tricorder in my office. I have action figures and comics and scholarly books about it. I own signed photographs of Worf and Sulu and Q, several original scripts, have met Spock and Scotty, even sent a sonnet written on the occasion of the latter's death to the stars, but I had never met Kirk, except insofar as being raised by him. Last year, eighty years into my father's life, two into his battle with brain disease, that changed. I, my wife, my son, my oldest sister, and my niece took my dad to meet William Shatner at the *Trek* Expo in Tulsa Oklahoma, not so terribly far from the Enterprise I sat in years ago as a young geek—the Enterprise that, like my father, is no longer there. I wanted to have a picture taken of me, my Captain, and my Colonel.

My wife, wonder that she is, approached Shatner to let him know the situation, told him about my father, about his Alzheimer's, and Shatner—himself an actor whose most recent role was a man suffering the same disease—said he understood, asked that we be moved to the front of the line, offered my father the most sincere empathy I could have imagined. My father—now no longer a father, no longer a husband, no longer NASA prospect or pilot or prodigy or, sometimes, even a man—this body that still *looked* like my father approached Shatner and spoke.

To this actor he'd never met, my father said, "Do you remember me?"

Shatner, smiling kindly, replied, "Why, yes. Do you know

who I am?"

My father, my oldest god, my avatar, my archetype, my conscience and my Kirk, said, "No."

Bryan D. Dietrich
February 2010

About the Poet

Bryan D. Dietrich is the author of a book-length study on comics, *Wonder Woman Unbound*, and six books of poems. He is also co-editor of *Drawn to Marvel*, an anthology of superhero poetry.

His poetry has been published in *The New Yorker, The Nation, Poetry, Ploughshares, Harvard Review, Yale Review*, and many other journals. Bryan has won numerous awards for his work, and been nominated multiple times for both the Pushcart and the Pulitzer.

He lives in Wichita, Kansas with his wife, Gina, their son, Nick, and a cat they call Darkness.
Visit his website at: http://www.bryandietrich.com/